I Don't Deserve to Have Money

I Don't Deserve to Have Money

Matthew Petchinsky

1

I Don't Deserve to Have Money

By: Matthew Petchinsky

Disclaimer:

This book, *I Don't Deserve to Have Money*, is a trauma-informed emotional guide created to help readers explore and understand feelings of financial undeservingness. It is designed for personal reflection, education, and empowerment, not as a replacement for therapy, counseling, or medical treatment. The material within draws upon psychological, emotional, and spiritual frameworks to help readers develop a healthier inner relationship with money, self-worth, and abundance.

Readers are encouraged to use the exercises, reflections, and concepts presented here as supportive tools alongside—never instead of—professional guidance where needed. If you have experienced trauma, financial abuse, or mental health challenges, consider reading this book in partnership with a licensed therapist, counselor, or financial therapist who can provide personalized care.

The author does not claim to diagnose, treat, or cure any psychological or financial condition. All examples, stories, and strategies are offered for educational purposes and are meant to inspire deeper awareness, self-compassion, and healing around money shame and worthiness. Each reader's journey is unique; progress may vary based on personal readiness, circumstances, and access to resources.

By engaging with this material, you acknowledge personal responsibility for your choices and interpretations, and you understand that transformation begins with curiosity, safety, and self-kindness—not self-blame.

Introduction:

You're not broken — you're bruised.

That simple truth reframes everything about your relationship with money, self-worth, and the invisible ceilings that keep abundance out of reach. For too long, you may have blamed yourself for not being "disciplined enough," "savvy enough," or "motivated enough." Yet beneath the surface, this has never been about budgeting or hustle. It's about *belonging* — the deep, quiet sense of whether you feel you deserve to have your needs met, to feel safe, and to live with ease.

When we say, "I don't deserve to have money," what we often mean is, "I was taught that comfort, rest, and support are for other people." These are the hidden lessons of survival. They come from childhood environments where love was conditional, where receiving was labeled greedy, or where scarcity was worn like armor. Over time, the nervous system learns to associate money with guilt, fear, or danger. So even as you consciously wish to thrive, an unconscious part of you pulls away — protecting you from what it believes will hurt.

This book is your invitation to meet that part of yourself not with force, but with compassion. Together, we'll trace where your resistance to money began — the moments of shame, rejection, or invisibility that rewired your sense of worth. You'll learn how emotional bruises create financial blocks, and why attempts to "fix" your money situation often fail when the root is unhealed trauma, not poor discipline.

From there, we rebuild — gently, intentionally, from the soul outward. You'll discover practical and emotional frameworks for re-establishing your right to receive. We'll examine how self-trust, boundaries, and nervous system regulation can quietly restore your capacity to hold abundance without fear. And you'll practice small, radical acts of allowing — accepting help, saying yes to joy, and no longer apologizing for your existence.

This is not a book about manifesting through wishful thinking, nor is it a financial strategy manual. It's a healing codex for self-permission — a guide to reclaiming your inherent worth as someone who is allowed to prosper, rest, and be supported. Because when you heal the part of you that believes money is not meant for you, you begin to open every other door that life has kept closed.

You are not here to earn your worth.
You are here to remember it — and to receive accordingly.

Chapter 1: The Origin of "I Don't Deserve"

Unlearning the emotional inheritance of unworthiness.

Every belief has a birthplace. Before the sentence "I don't deserve to have money" was ever spoken aloud, it existed as a feeling — a subtle contraction in your body, a tightening in your chest, or a small, guilty pause every time something good came your way. This belief did not emerge in isolation. It was *taught*, *modeled*, or *absorbed* by the emotional environment that raised you. To heal it, we must first trace it back to where it began.

The Emotional Blueprint We Inherit

Children learn about money long before they can count. They learn through tone, tension, and silence — the way adults speak about bills, the sigh before a purchase, the arguments whispered at night. These moments imprint messages that shape our adult relationship with wealth. If money was associated with stress, you may have internalized that safety and prosperity cannot coexist. If someone in your home said, "People like us don't have that kind of luck," the phrase might have settled deep within you as a rule, not an opinion. Over time, it became an identity: *I am not one of the ones who get to have more.*

You may have grown up around self-sacrifice being glorified, where generosity meant depletion and rest was earned only through exhaustion. In such systems, worth is measured by suffering. It's no wonder that later in life, receiving feels suspicious — almost sinful.

Shame as an Unseen Currency

At the root of undeservingness is *shame*. Shame is the belief that something about you disqualifies you from goodness. It is quieter than guilt and more corrosive than fear. While guilt says, "I did something bad," shame whispers, "I *am* bad."

When money enters this equation, every paycheck, gift, or opportunity becomes a moral test. Do I deserve this? Did I earn this? Am I enough? The nervous system, conditioned to equate love with deprivation, interprets abundance as unsafe — and subconsciously repels it.

Family Narratives That Rewrite Your Self-Value

Families often carry inherited scripts about money:

- *"We're just not those kinds of people."*
- *"Hard work is the only way to survive."*
- *"Rich people are greedy."*
- *"Don't ask for too much — you'll jinx it."*

Each of these phrases seems harmless until you recognize how they shape identity. They subtly teach that to stay loyal, loved, or safe within your family system, you must share its limitations. To outgrow scarcity can feel like betrayal.

Cultural and Societal Conditioning

Beyond family, society reinforces these wounds. Many cultures moralize poverty and villainize wealth. You are praised for enduring struggle but judged for receiving ease. Entire economies rely on people who feel undeserving — those who overwork, undercharge, and apologize for wanting better.

To reclaim your worth is an act of quiet rebellion. It's saying, "I can be humble *and* abundant. I can be kind *and* comfortable."

The Nervous System's Role in "Deservingness"

Undeservingness is not just a thought — it's a physiological state. If your body associates wealth or success with danger (rejection, envy, abandonment), your system will unconsciously avoid it. You might self-sabotage opportunities or dismiss gifts as "too much."

Healing begins with safety. You cannot reprogram your worth if your body is still braced for punishment. Somatic awareness — noticing where tension lives when you think of receiving — is often the first doorway to freedom.

The Truth Beneath the Fear

When we say "I don't deserve," what we often mean is, "I fear what will happen if I *do*." Will people leave me? Will they see me differently? Will I owe something I cannot repay? Beneath the undeserving story lies a deeper one about connection, trust, and identity.

This chapter invites you to name that fear — not to judge it, but to understand its origins. Because when you trace the bruise, you begin to heal it.

10 Journal Prompts to Explore Your "I Don't Deserve Money" Origin

Use these prompts slowly. Let your body, not just your mind, answer.

1. What is your earliest memory of hearing adults talk about money? How did it make you feel?
2. When someone gave you something as a child, how did you respond — with gratitude, guilt, or refusal?
3. What phrases about money did you hear repeatedly growing up?
4. Did you ever witness conflict, silence, or fear surrounding finances in your home?
5. Who in your family seemed most "deserving" of money? Who seemed least deserving?
6. What emotions surface in your body when you think of receiving money without earning it?
7. When did you first connect money with moral worth (good vs. bad people)?
8. What cultural or community beliefs shaped your views of wealth and poverty?
9. Can you recall a moment you rejected abundance — a gift, opportunity, or compliment — because it felt "too much"?
10. What might happen if you truly believed you deserved to be supported?

Closing Reflection: Returning to the Source

Every bruise has a story. Yours may begin in whispered arguments, unspoken fears, or inherited struggle — but it does not have to end there. You are now the caretaker of your own emotional lineage. By recognizing where your undeservingness began, you loosen its hold on the present.

Sit quietly and place your hand over your heart. Whisper:

"I no longer need to earn the right to exist in safety, comfort, or peace."

This chapter has opened the wound gently.

Chapter 2: How Abuse & Neglect Shape Deservingness

Understanding the emotional architecture of financial self-denial.

You don't just wake up one day believing you don't deserve good things — that belief is *taught through experience*. Abuse and neglect do not merely wound the heart; they rewrite the very algorithms of self-worth. When love, attention, or safety were inconsistently given — or outright withheld — your nervous system learned an impossible equation: **"To stay safe, I must need less."**

This chapter explores how emotional neglect, manipulation, and trauma create invisible contracts that carry into adulthood — the kind that tell you not to ask for too much, not to celebrate your wins, not to shine too brightly. And, most insidiously, not to receive.

The Hidden Economics of Abuse

Every abusive dynamic has its own economy. Love, approval, and safety are treated like scarce commodities you must earn. One wrong word, one unmet expectation, and the cost is withdrawal, silence, or punishment.

In such environments, children learn that *receiving* comes at a price. When affection is transactional, money becomes dangerous — a symbol of power imbalance. You might unconsciously believe that having more will make you a target, that abundance will bring resentment or retaliation.

Over time, you internalize the logic of your abusers: if something good happens to you, you must have done something wrong. So you begin to preemptively deprive yourself — emotionally and financially — before anyone else can. This is the cycle of *self-imposed poverty*: punishing yourself before the world has the chance.

Neglect as the Silent Teacher

Neglect doesn't always come as violence. Sometimes, it's the ache of what *never came at all*: the parent who never noticed, the partner who never listened, the system that never cared.

In neglect, a child learns that needs are inconvenient. Asking leads to disappointment. Wanting too much means being too much.

So the body learns to shrink. It learns to associate quietness with safety, invisibility with survival.

As an adult, this conditioning mutates into financial self-erasure. You might downplay your achievements, undercharge for your work, or sabotage opportunities because visibility still feels like danger. Subconsciously, you may believe that thriving would make you lose love — or worse, draw harm.

Shame and the Inverted Mirror of Value

Abuse mirrors you back through distortion. You're told you're selfish when you assert a boundary, ungrateful when you need rest, lazy when you pause to breathe. Eventually, you stop questioning the mirror and start questioning yourself.

This distortion doesn't disappear with time. It becomes internalized shame — a reflex that fires whenever something good tries to enter your life. Shame whispers, *"You haven't earned this. Someone else needs it more. You're not the type who gets to have that."*

Money, in this sense, becomes a moral test. To receive it feels like stealing. To want it feels dirty. So, you unconsciously recreate scarcity — because that feels familiar, and familiarity feels safe.

Trauma Bonds and the Loyalty to Suffering

When abuse or neglect define your formative years, a strange loyalty forms — to pain itself. Your nervous system learns that suffering equals connection. You might stay attached to hardship because it reminds you of love's earliest form.

Breaking this bond is terrifying. Part of you believes that leaving struggle behind means leaving *belonging* behind. This is why financial healing often triggers grief. You're not just learning to receive — you're mourning the years you believed you had to starve to be loved.

How Trauma Shapes the "Deservingness Reflex"

Deservingness is not a conscious decision; it's an embodied reflex. When abuse teaches you that attention equals harm, your body may instinctively flinch at praise or opportunity. When neglect teaches you that silence equals safety, your system may shut down when someone offers help.

Rebuilding this reflex takes time. You cannot think your way into worthiness. You must *feel* your way into it — one safe moment at a time. Healing begins by re-teaching your body that good things can arrive *and stay* without punishment following.

Healing the Scarcity Identity

The belief "I don't deserve to have money" is often a symptom of something deeper: *I learned that my needs caused pain.*

To dissolve that belief, you must gently contradict it through experience.

- Allow yourself to accept something small — a compliment, a meal, a day off — without repayment.
- Practice holding comfort without apology.
- Surround yourself with people who celebrate your receiving instead of demanding your sacrifice.

Each act of allowing becomes a tiny revolution against your conditioning — proof that you can be loved *and* provided for.

10 Journal Prompts to Explore How Abuse & Neglect Shaped Your Deservingness

1. When you were growing up, what happened when you expressed a need or desire?
2. How did the adults around you respond to your success or joy?
3. Were there times when receiving something good made you feel guilty or afraid?
4. How were love and attention "earned" in your family or relationships?
5. What were you taught—explicitly or silently—about people who have money?
6. When did you first equate self-denial with safety?
7. What parts of you still believe that being small or invisible keeps you protected?
8. How do you feel in your body when someone gives you a gift or compliment?
9. Who taught you that needing less made you more lovable?
10. What would it feel like to no longer associate receiving with danger?

Closing Reflection: The End of the Survival Contract

Abuse and neglect forge invisible contracts: *"If I stay small, I'll stay safe."* But every contract can be rewritten. You are no longer the child who had to choose between love and security. You are the adult who can hold both.

Tonight, place your hand over your chest and breathe into the words:

"I release the belief that suffering is loyalty. I am safe to receive."

The bruise of undeservingness does not define you — it identifies where love once failed to reach. In healing it, you do not erase your past; you reclaim the power it once stole.

Chapter 3: The Fear of Being Seen with Wealth

How visibility, judgment, and safety intertwine in the subconscious mind.

To heal financial undeservingness, we must face one of its most persistent roots: **the fear of being seen.**

For many trauma survivors, visibility feels like exposure. To be seen is to be vulnerable — and vulnerability, in the past, meant danger. When money or success enters the picture, that fear doesn't disappear; it evolves. Wealth becomes a spotlight you're not sure you can survive standing under.

This chapter explores why so many people who have experienced emotional neglect, rejection, or control develop an instinctive aversion to being visibly comfortable. It's not greed or guilt you're afraid of — it's *what happens when others notice you have more.*

The Nervous System and the Spotlight Reflex

Every nervous system has a threshold for attention. If your childhood experiences taught you that being noticed led to criticism, punishment, or jealousy, your body may still equate visibility with risk.

Now, as an adult, that reflex translates into financial invisibility. You might:

- Downplay your success so others don't feel bad.
- Decline opportunities that could elevate your income.
- Give away what you earn before you can enjoy it.
- Keep your lifestyle modest even when you can afford more.

This is not self-sabotage — it's *self-protection.* The body remembers what the mind rationalizes away. When you were younger, safety depended on staying small, quiet, and unnoticed. Your nervous system has simply kept that promise.

The Cultural Fear of "Too Much"

Society reinforces this wound through shame-based conditioning. People are praised for surviving poverty but criticized for thriving past it. Wealth is seen as suspicious, even when earned ethically. Those who rise are accused of forgetting where they came from; those who stay small are deemed humble and "real."

If you grew up in a community where everyone struggled, wealth can feel like exile. To prosper may mean to leave people behind — or worse, to become the kind of person who once hurt you. So you create an unconscious compromise: "I'll allow just enough to survive, but never enough to be envied."

This is why you can work hard and still find your income plateauing. Your inner system is trying to protect your belonging by keeping your visibility low.

The Envy Wound: When Abundance Feels Dangerous

Envy is a primal social trigger. When someone resents your success, it activates the old fear of persecution — the child who was bullied for standing out, the teen who was mocked for trying. The message becomes clear: *Attention brings attack.*

So even if you consciously crave prosperity, another part of you flinches. You may hide purchases, feel shame when celebrating milestones, or secretly fear being "found out" for having something others don't.

This is the **envy wound** — the internalized belief that joy must be hidden to stay safe. It's a leftover defense mechanism, but it costs you peace and authenticity.

Trauma's Inversion of Worth: The Safety of Scarcity

When safety has always come through deprivation, abundance feels foreign. You may not fear money itself, but the *changes* it might bring — the loss of control, the shifts in relationships, the expectations that follow.

Many survivors unconsciously equate scarcity with safety because it's familiar. Scarcity asks nothing of you. It keeps you invisible. It protects you from envy, judgment, and confrontation. But it also keeps you small, anxious, and tired.

To heal, you must re-train your body to recognize that *being seen can be safe.* The path forward isn't to flaunt wealth; it's to inhabit it without fear — to exist comfortably in your own light without apology.

The Myth of the "Good Poor Person"

Deep within collective conditioning lies a false binary: the *good poor person* versus the *corrupt rich person.* Many who were raised around moralized poverty internalize this dichotomy — believing that having less makes you more virtuous.

But this myth robs you of balance. Wealth, in itself, is neutral. It magnifies the integrity or dysfunction already present. It can be used to heal, build, and sustain — or to control, exploit, and harm. Refusing money does not make you pure; it often just keeps you powerless.

Releasing this myth means understanding that you can be *ethical, kind, generous, and prosperous at the same time.* Your wealth can be an extension of your healing, not a betrayal of it.

Healing the Visibility Wound

Visibility healing happens through incremental exposure, not force. You can't jump from shame to shining overnight; your body won't let you. Instead:

- Start by acknowledging the sensations that arise when you think about being wealthy or celebrated.
- Notice the physical tension — the tight throat, shallow breath, or flutter in the gut.
- Breathe into them and remind yourself, *"This is old safety, not current danger."*
- Practice being seen in safe environments: share small wins with trusted people, express gratitude openly, or celebrate without minimizing your success.

Each act of being visible without consequence rewires your nervous system's associations. Over time, you'll notice that receiving praise or money no longer feels like exposure — it feels like recognition.

The Sacred Right to Shine

Deservingness and visibility are intertwined. You cannot believe you deserve abundance while hiding from being seen. To claim your worth is to let yourself exist fully — not as a shadow in someone else's story, but as the author of your own.

You have survived invisibility. You have built strength in the quiet. Now, it's time to learn how to *be seen without being afraid.* Because wealth isn't just about money — it's about the freedom to stand in your truth without apology.

10 Journal Prompts to Explore the Fear of Being Seen with Wealth

1. When was the first time being noticed felt unsafe for you?
2. How did people around you respond when someone in your family or community achieved success?
3. What do you fear others might think if you became visibly wealthy?
4. In what ways have you hidden your success, comfort, or progress to keep others comfortable?
5. What sensations arise in your body when you imagine being fully seen and celebrated?
6. Who taught you that having more makes you less lovable or "real"?
7. What identities (humble, quiet, struggling) feel safer to you than being prosperous?
8. If wealth didn't mean losing belonging, how might you show up differently?
9. How can you begin to associate visibility with safety and connection instead of danger?
10. What small act could you take this week to let yourself be seen in your abundance — even a little?

Closing Reflection: Letting the Light Touch You

The fear of being seen is not vanity — it is survival instinct. But survival is no longer your only mission. You are allowed to step into visibility without expecting punishment. You are allowed to receive and be witnessed in your receiving.

Tonight, whisper softly to yourself:

"I am safe to shine. My light harms no one. My abundance threatens nothing."

Being seen in your wealth is not arrogance — it is authenticity. It shows the world what healing looks like when shame no longer runs the show. In being seen, you give others permission to rise too.

Chapter 4: How to Receive Without Fear

Letting money, support, and care enter your life without mistaking them for danger.

Receiving sounds simple — until it isn't.
For those shaped by trauma, rejection, or chronic self-denial, the act of receiving can feel like standing in front of a tidal wave. Even kindness can register as threat. Support can trigger guilt. Money can awaken anxiety. Because somewhere in your history, receiving came with a cost — rejection, ridicule, obligation, or loss.

This chapter will help you understand why your body confuses receiving with danger and how to rewire that reflex. You'll learn how to feel safe with abundance, to accept help without shame, and to let love, wealth, and care *stay* once they arrive.

The Physiology of Fear Around Receiving

Your body doesn't differentiate between emotional and physical threat. When you receive something — praise, money, affection — your nervous system scans for danger. If your early experiences associated gifts with control ("I gave you this, so now you owe me") or love with conditions ("You only get this when you're good"), the body learned that receiving equals vulnerability.

That's why generosity can feel like pressure, and success can feel like exposure.
Your heart races, your chest tightens, your mind floods with intrusive thoughts:
What do they want from me?
Will this be taken away?
Do I really deserve this?

You're not ungrateful — you're *protective.* Your nervous system is trying to keep you from reliving old harm. The key is to retrain it to recognize that receiving can now mean *safety,* not risk.

Why the Wounded Self Rejects Support

The part of you that resists help is often the same part that survived abandonment. When no one came to your rescue, you learned self-reliance as armor. You built an identity around not needing anyone — because needing was dangerous.

But independence born from trauma isn't freedom; it's isolation disguised as strength.

When you reject help, gifts, or opportunities, you're not protecting your autonomy — you're reenacting old loneliness. Healing means allowing others (and the universe itself) to give to you *without fear that it will disappear or demand repayment.*

Receiving doesn't erase your resilience. It completes it. It teaches your system that strength and softness can coexist.

The Hidden Guilt of Prosperity

Many people carry unspoken guilt about wanting or having more. You might feel that every dollar you earn takes away from someone else, or that abundance is selfish when others are struggling. But scarcity isn't solved by deprivation — it's perpetuated by it.

When you let yourself receive, you expand the field of what's possible for everyone. You model wholeness. You show others that it's safe to have their needs met without shame. Refusing money or support doesn't make you generous — it makes you tired, small, and disconnected from the natural flow of reciprocity that keeps life in motion.

Money, like breath, must circulate. You can't give what you don't allow yourself to hold.

Safety Practice #1: Slow Receiving

Start small. Let your body acclimate to the feeling of being given to.

- When someone compliments you, pause before deflecting. Simply say, "Thank you." Feel what happens in your chest, your breath, your shoulders.
- When someone offers help, notice your first impulse. Do you want to say, "No, I've got it"? Try instead, "That would really help, thank you."
- When unexpected money appears — a refund, a bonus, a gift — resist the urge to immediately spend or "balance" it. Let it sit. Let it *exist* without justification.

Slow receiving trains your nervous system that good things can arrive without punishment following. The more you stay present through that discomfort, the more safety you build around abundance.

Safety Practice #2: Rewriting the "Cost Narrative"

If you were raised to believe everything comes with strings attached, receiving freely will feel impossible. You may unconsciously think:

- "If I take this, I'll owe them."
- "They'll expect something back."
- "It's safer not to depend on anyone."

Write these fears down. Then beside each one, write: *That was true then. It is not true now.*

This simple reframe interrupts trauma-time thinking — the assumption that the past is still happening. You begin to separate historical danger from present safety.

Remind yourself: **Healthy giving has no debt. True support has no trap.**

Safety Practice #3: Somatic Grounding When Receiving

Receiving activates the same survival systems that respond to threat. To calm them:

1. **Ground physically.** Feel your feet on the floor. Press your toes down. Imagine roots stabilizing you.
2. **Anchor with breath.** Inhale slowly through your nose for four counts. Exhale for six. Longer exhales tell your body, *I am safe.*
3. **Name the feeling aloud.** "This is anxiety, not danger." "This is excitement, not guilt." Naming helps the brain reclassify the sensation as tolerable.
4. **Visualize containment.** Picture your body as a vessel big enough to hold the gift, the money, or the care being offered — without leaking it away.

Over time, these practices rebuild the somatic safety that trauma once stole.

Reframing Receiving as Sacred Exchange

Healthy receiving isn't passive — it's participation in life's circulation.

When you allow yourself to receive, you're affirming that the world can meet you halfway. You're saying, *"I am open to connection, not just contribution."*

Imagine money, love, and care as rivers — not trophies. They're meant to flow. By blocking your inflow, you block the collective ecosystem of generosity itself.

Receiving is spiritual reciprocity. It's how the universe breathes: in, out, in, out. You wouldn't inhale without exhaling. Don't give without allowing yourself to take in.

Practical Repatterning: The Deservingness Daily Ritual

Create a simple daily ritual to retrain your system toward acceptance:

1. **Morning:** Speak this affirmation aloud — "I am open to safe receiving today."
2. **Throughout the day:** When someone offers help, pause and ask yourself, *Is this generosity or manipulation?* (If it's healthy, accept it.)
3. **Evening:** Write one sentence about what you received — material or emotional — and how it felt in your body.
4. **Weekly:** Treat yourself to something small without guilt — a meal, an item, rest — and notice how your system responds.

Consistency, not scale, heals. You are teaching your nervous system that good things can enter without danger attached.

10 Journal Prompts: Learning to Receive Without Fear

1. When was the first time receiving something made you feel unsafe or indebted?
2. How did your caregivers or partners react when you accepted help or gifts?
3. What emotions surface when you think about people giving to you freely?
4. How do you typically respond to compliments, money, or assistance?
5. What beliefs have you internalized about what it means to "deserve" support?
6. What is your body's first physical reaction when you receive — tightening, warmth, numbness, tension?
7. How might life feel different if receiving felt natural and safe?
8. What would "safe support" look like for you right now?
9. Who in your life models healthy, unapologetic receiving? What can you learn from them?
10. What would you need to tell your nervous system today to let more goodness in?

Closing Reflection: Opening the Door and Staying Home

Receiving is not weakness — it's the natural rhythm of wholeness returning. You've spent years surviving by keeping the door half-closed, scanning for danger. Now, you're learning that safety can coexist with plenty.

Money can flow in without control following. Support can arrive without betrayal hiding beneath it. Love can be offered without demand.

Sit quietly for a moment and breathe into this truth:

"It is safe for me to be supported. It is safe for me to have more than enough."

You are not here to earn worthiness — only to remember it. The universe has always been trying to give to you. Healing means learning, at last, to say yes.

Chapter 5: The Right to Receive and Rest

Healing the belief that rest and abundance must be earned.

You have the right to receive. You have the right to rest.

These statements may seem simple — yet for many, they're among the hardest truths to accept. Because in a world built on constant output, your worth is often measured by exhaustion. You were taught to prove your value through overwork, to apologize for ease, and to equate burnout with success.

But deservingness is not earned through depletion. The capacity to receive and the permission to rest are not luxuries — they are the foundation of wholeness. This chapter explores how exhaustion, scarcity, and emotional unworthiness intertwine — and how reclaiming your right to rest is the final frontier of learning to receive.

The False Religion of Productivity

From an early age, many of us were conditioned to believe that stillness equals laziness. "Work hard, and you'll be rewarded" became a moral code — a creed that framed rest as indulgence and struggle as virtue.

Over time, this mindset trains the nervous system to equate activity with safety. To stop moving feels like falling behind. To rest feels like failing.

This conditioning becomes internalized capitalism of the soul — a system where your sense of worth rises and falls with your output. The result is spiritual fatigue: an inability to pause, breathe, or feel safe doing nothing.

Receiving, in this paradigm, feels undeserved because you were never allowed to exist without effort. The moment you stop striving, guilt rushes in to fill the silence.

Trauma's War with Stillness

For those with histories of chaos, neglect, or abuse, rest can feel dangerous. Stillness means you can't predict what happens next. Activity — even meaningless activity — offers a sense of control.

You may notice that the moment you relax, intrusive thoughts or anxiety arise. That's not weakness; it's your body bracing for impact. It remembers the times when "peace" was only a pause before the next explosion.

Learning to rest safely means teaching your nervous system that calm can exist without catastrophe. It's about creating safety in stillness — to remind your body that the storm has passed.

The Scarcity Loop: When Enough Is Never Enough

The inability to rest is tied to the belief that there is never enough — not enough money, time, energy, or worth. You hustle harder, not because you want to, but because you're terrified of losing everything if you stop.

But exhaustion doesn't create safety — it recreates fear.

Rest is what interrupts the scarcity loop. It tells your body, "I am safe even when I am not producing." It reminds your mind that you are not a machine. Rest is the reset button that abundance requires — because receiving requires openness, and tension blocks flow.

To rest is to tell the universe: *"I trust that I can stop and still be supported."*

Reclaiming the Birthright of Ease

Every living thing rests. The sun sets, the tide retreats, trees shed their leaves, the body sleeps. Rest is not withdrawal — it's participation in life's rhythm.

Your right to rest is inherent; it existed before anyone told you to earn it. You are allowed to lie down before the work is done. You are allowed to receive without repayment. You are allowed to feel full without guilt.

Ease is not laziness — it's alignment. When you allow yourself to rest, you stop pushing life and start flowing with it. You return to the natural rhythm your spirit always knew.

The Connection Between Rest and Receiving

Receiving requires openness. You cannot open when you are clenched in survival mode.

The exhausted body repels abundance because it's too busy bracing for loss. When you rest, your nervous system signals safety, which in turn signals receptivity.

This is why people who prioritize rest often find opportunities, ideas, and blessings arriving effortlessly. It's not magic — it's physiology. Rest activates the parasympathetic nervous system, which governs digestion, healing, creativity, and trust. When your body believes it's safe, it finally lets good things *in.*

Rest isn't the absence of work — it's the soil where your worth takes root.

Learning to Receive Rest Without Guilt

Rest can feel uncomfortable at first, especially if guilt immediately follows relaxation. You may hear inner voices that say:

- "You haven't earned this."
- "Other people have it harder."
- "You're wasting time."

These voices aren't truth; they're echoes of old systems of control — family, culture, capitalism, trauma.
Try replacing them with new internal language:

- "Resting is repair, not weakness."
- "My body and mind deserve recovery."
- "The world benefits when I am restored."

Rest isn't a withdrawal from contribution — it's preparation for sustainable giving. You cannot pour from a cracked vessel.

Practical Rest Rituals for Receptivity

Create deliberate practices that train your body to equate rest with safety and receiving:

1. **Micro-Rests:** Schedule 5–10 minute intervals during the day where you do nothing — no phone, no productivity, just breathing.
2. **Permission Statements:** Before resting, say aloud, "It's safe for me to rest." This verbal cue rewires guilt associations.
3. **Restful Receiving:** When you rest, visualize light or abundance entering your body. Imagine it filling the spaces where tension used to live.
4. **Evening Surrender:** End each day with one sentence of release: *"I did enough today. I am enough even when I stop."*

Over time, these rituals replace restlessness with receptivity — allowing your nervous system to see rest as a doorway, not a danger.

The Wealth of Stillness

Rest and receiving are not opposites — they are partners. Wealth, at its deepest level, is not accumulation; it's *capacity.* The more rested you are, the greater your capacity to hold abundance, kindness, and clarity. When you are depleted, even blessings feel heavy. When you are rested, even small gifts feel vast.

The ability to rest deeply is the highest form of wealth — because it means you finally trust that life continues to move even when you pause. You are no longer hustling for permission to exist.

10 Journal Prompts: Reclaiming Your Right to Receive and Rest

1. What were you taught about rest growing up? Who modeled it — or who never did?
2. How do you feel when you stop working or slow down? What sensations arise?
3. What beliefs make you feel you must earn comfort, money, or ease?
4. When do you feel most deserving — and what must you do to feel that way?
5. What fears surface when you imagine taking a full day off without guilt?
6. How does exhaustion make you feel "safe" or "productive"?
7. What does genuine rest feel like in your body — heavy, light, still, or free?
8. How can you make small daily pauses feel sacred instead of selfish?
9. What would your life look like if you fully trusted that rest invites more, not less?
10. What new definition of "deserving" would allow you to rest without explanation?

Closing Reflection: You Are Worthy of Ease

You are not alive to prove your worth through exhaustion.
You are not required to earn rest, affection, or abundance.

You are allowed to lie in sunlight without apology. You are allowed to let money arrive without panic. You are allowed to sleep without shame.

Close your eyes and whisper:
"I am worthy of stillness. I am worthy of support. I am worthy of ease."

In this quiet permission, the nervous system loosens, the soul exhales, and the flow of life returns.

Receiving and resting are not the end of your healing — they are the evidence that healing has begun.

Chapter 6: Rebuilding the Worthiness Core

Becoming the person who feels safe, capable, and deserving of abundance.

At the center of every financial, emotional, and relational transformation lies one truth: **you must rebuild your sense of worth.**
You can learn every manifestation practice, every budgeting method, every self-help strategy — but if your inner architecture is still shaped by the belief *"I am not enough,"* everything you create will collapse under the weight of self-doubt.

Rebuilding the worthiness core isn't about ego or entitlement. It's about reclaiming the sacred truth that you were born worthy — not because of what you do, but because you exist. This chapter will help you reconstruct that truth from the inside out: psychologically, emotionally, and spiritually. You will learn to feel at home within your own value again.

The Core Wound of Unworthiness

Unworthiness is not a character flaw; it is a learned trauma response. Somewhere in your past, worth became conditional — tied to achievement, approval, or obedience. You may have been praised only when you performed, loved only when you pleased, or noticed only when you struggled.

Over time, this creates an inner split between the **performing self** (the one who earns approval) and the **authentic self** (the one who quietly wonders if love would exist without performance).
That split breeds chronic insecurity. You begin to chase validation externally because the internal source has been forgotten. The worthiness core cracks — and every part of life built upon it begins to wobble.

Rebuilding that foundation means returning to the truth that worth was *never lost*, only buried beneath layers of survival.

Recognizing the False Architecture of Self-Worth

When worthiness is externalized, it becomes a fragile structure built on shifting ground. It takes the form of:

- **Perfectionism:** "If I do everything right, I'll finally be safe."
- **People-pleasing:** "If I keep everyone happy, I'll be loved."
- **Overworking:** "If I never stop producing, I'll stay valuable."
- **Undercharging or overgiving:** "If I make myself indispensable, I won't be abandoned."

Each of these patterns is an attempt to stabilize worth through control. But control doesn't heal insecurity — it feeds it. The more you try to earn what was always meant to be inherent, the further you drift from peace.

Rebuilding your core begins by dismantling these false pillars one by one and learning to anchor worth within, not around you.

Reclaiming the Body as the First Temple of Worth

The body holds the memory of worth — or its absence.

If you've lived in chronic stress or shame, your body may have learned to tighten, shrink, or disappear. The first step in rebuilding worthiness is to **reinhabit your body**.

You cannot feel deserving while disconnected from the vessel that carries you.

Start by noticing how your body responds to the idea of "I am enough." Do you feel warmth? Resistance? Numbness? That reaction tells you exactly where the repair must begin.

Worthiness is not a thought to repeat; it's a feeling to embody.

Rebuilding it means learning to inhabit your physical presence with safety, self-respect, and care — feeding yourself properly, sleeping deeply, moving gently, and speaking to your body as if it were a beloved child rather than an obstacle.

Emotional Repair: From Self-Rejection to Self-Trust

The worthiness core thrives on one emotion above all: **trust.** Abuse, neglect, and disappointment erode that trust — in others and in yourself. You start to doubt your instincts, dismiss your needs, and outsource your authority.

To rebuild self-trust:

1. **Keep promises to yourself**, even small ones. Integrity restores confidence.
2. **Listen to discomfort** instead of overriding it. Your body is always communicating boundaries and truth.
3. **Forgive your past self** for how they survived. Shame keeps the worthiness core fractured; compassion fuses it back together.

Every time you honor your inner signals, you prove to yourself that you are safe in your own care — and worth begins to feel like home again.

Reframing Worth as Birthright, Not Achievement

A powerful shift happens when you realize: **You were worthy before you ever achieved a thing.**

No amount of success adds to that worth, and no failure subtracts from it.

Think of worthiness as a frequency you're born tuned to — but life's noise can detune you. Rebuilding doesn't mean creating something new; it means remembering your original setting.

You don't have to *become* enough. You only have to stop believing you weren't.

Begin practicing this reframe daily:

"My worth is not up for negotiation. It is the constant beneath every changing circumstance."

When you live from this truth, you stop performing for belonging — and start participating in it.

The Link Between Worth and Wealth

Money mirrors your sense of self. If you secretly believe you are unworthy, you will unconsciously limit how much you allow yourself to receive, earn, or keep.

Wealth is not about greed — it's about capacity. The more you believe you are worthy, the more your nervous system can safely hold abundance.

When your worthiness core is fractured, money leaks through guilt, overspending, or self-sabotage. But when it's strong, you stop apologizing for having enough. You no longer equate comfort with danger or success with shame.

Rebuilding worth is rebuilding your energetic container — allowing you to hold wealth without fear, visibility without shame, and success without self-abandonment.

Spiritual Integration: The Soul's Memory of Value

Beyond psychology, there is a spiritual truth: worthiness is woven into your being. It is not learned — it is *remembered.*

Every time you reconnect with your own presence — through breath, nature, art, or prayerful silence — you remind your soul of its inherent belonging in the web of life.

You are not an accident. You are not a cosmic clerical error waiting to justify your existence. You are the proof that the universe wanted to experience itself as *you.*

When you remember that, the entire architecture of self-doubt collapses.

Worthiness becomes not something you build, but something you uncover — like gold beneath layers of dust.

Practices for Strengthening the Worthiness Core

To keep the reconstruction solid, engage in these restorative practices daily or weekly:

1. **The Worth Statement Ritual:** Stand before a mirror and say, "I am worthy of love, rest, money, and peace — not because I earned them, but because I exist." Repeat until your voice feels steady.
2. **Gratitude for Self:** Each night, list three things you *gave* yourself that day — patience, nourishment, rest, forgiveness.
3. **The Boundary Breath:** Inhale with the words "I belong to myself." Exhale with "My energy is mine to direct."
4. **Inner Child Dialogue:** Speak to your younger self as a guardian, not a critic. Let them know they never had to earn your care.
5. **Rest as Ritual:** Schedule rest as if it were a meeting with your higher self — because it is.

Consistency re-teaches your subconscious that you are safe, loved, and enough.

10 Journal Prompts: Rebuilding Your Worthiness Core

1. When did you first learn that love or acceptance had to be earned?
2. What behaviors or achievements do you tie your worth to today?
3. How does your body react when you say, "I am enough"?
4. Which relationships have mirrored your unworthiness — and which have reflected your value?
5. What does unconditional self-worth look like in daily life, not just words?
6. How do you respond to mistakes — with punishment or compassion?
7. What would your life look like if you truly trusted your own decisions?
8. In what areas of your life do you still shrink or apologize for existing?
9. What new belief about your worth would feel revolutionary to live by?
10. How can you remind yourself, every day, that you deserve to be here fully?

Closing Reflection: The Return to Enough

You were never broken — only buried beneath the rubble of misunderstanding.

Rebuilding your worthiness core is not a single act; it's a lifelong devotion to remembering your true foundation.

Stand still for a moment and breathe:

"I am already enough. I have always been enough. My worth does not need proof — it needs recognition."

When you anchor into that truth, money flows differently, relationships soften, and rest becomes natural.

The core of worth is not built on striving — it's built on remembering.

And in that remembrance, you rise unshakable.

Appendix A: The Deservingness Mantra Deck

How to Use This Deck

The *Deservingness Mantra Deck* is designed as both a daily practice and an energetic recalibration tool. Each mantra rewires one fragment of unworthiness into embodied truth. You can:

- **Draw one card each morning** to set the tone for the day.
- **Repeat three mantras nightly** before bed to reinforce safety in rest and receiving.
- **Use them in meditation** — speak the phrase, breathe into your heart, and let the words land in your body rather than your mind.

Each statement affirms that receiving is your right, not a reward. Feel free to adapt the language — whisper it, write it, or carry it with you until it becomes your lived reality.

The 100 Deservingness Mantras

1. I am safe to receive good things.
2. My worth is not up for debate.
3. I no longer confuse comfort with danger.
4. Rest is my birthright, not a prize.
5. I can hold abundance without guilt.
6. I am not too much or too little — I am enough.
7. Money can love me without hurting me.
8. My body knows how to feel safe with ease.
9. I deserve to be supported simply because I exist.
10. My nervous system can learn peace again.
11. I am allowed to stop striving and still be worthy.
12. I welcome generosity without repayment.
13. I am open to being seen in my abundance.
14. Safety and success can coexist.

15. I do not have to earn what I am.
16. I allow wealth to arrive gently.
17. My rest repairs what work cannot.
18. I trust life to sustain me when I pause.
19. I can be powerful and peaceful at the same time.
20. I release the belief that suffering makes me moral.
21. My needs are sacred, not shameful.
22. I am learning to hold joy without flinching.
23. I let go of ancestral scarcity with gratitude.
24. Receiving is not greed — it is balance.
25. I am a worthy steward of abundance.
26. I allow love and money to flow freely through me.
27. Ease does not erase effort; it honors it.
28. I am safe to be comfortable.
29. My worth remains constant, even in rest.
30. I can thrive without betraying my past.
31. I no longer shrink to be safe.
32. I allow visibility without fear.
33. I release loyalty to exhaustion.
34. My pleasure is not a threat to anyone.
35. I am rebuilding trust in the world's kindness.
36. I can rest without proving anything.
37. I have permission to enjoy what I've created.
38. My abundance benefits everyone it touches.
39. Receiving replenishes me so I can give from overflow.
40. I am allowed to feel safe with stability.
41. My boundaries protect my worth, not diminish it.
42. I am free to unlearn deprivation.
43. I belong in rooms filled with light and opportunity.
44. I forgive myself for surviving through scarcity.
45. I can celebrate wealth without guilt.
46. I am worthy of softness and strength.
47. I release the reflex to decline help.

48. It is safe for others to care for me.
49. I no longer perform for permission.
50. I receive without apology.
51. I am safe when life is good.
52. I am open to miracles that feel calm, not chaotic.
53. Every cell of my body remembers abundance.
54. My worth existed before I learned fear.
55. I no longer carry shame about wanting more.
56. I let go of the idea that I must earn ease.
57. My soul was born deserving.
58. I honor my body's need for rest and replenishment.
59. I can receive love without owing it back.
60. My presence alone is valuable.
61. I am worthy of gentleness.
62. I am not behind; I am exactly where I need to be.
63. The universe delights in giving to me.
64. I allow myself to be held by life.
65. I no longer mistake chaos for connection.
66. Abundance is not a betrayal of my roots.
67. I receive compliments as truth, not traps.
68. I am safe to relax into prosperity.
69. My dreams deserve nourishment.
70. I can hold money without fear of loss.
71. I am learning to rest without resistance.
72. I am open to ease in all forms.
73. I forgive the part of me that feared having more.
74. I am worthy of care even when I'm not productive.
75. I am safe to stop fixing myself.
76. I am no longer at war with my needs.
77. I can be abundant and kind simultaneously.
78. I trust that I will not be punished for peace.
79. My inner child deserves stability and love.
80. My worth is not determined by my output.

81. I release scarcity thinking with every breath.
82. I am open to safe and sustainable wealth.
83. My well-being creates ripples of good in the world.
84. I am allowed to exhale without fear.
85. I rest because I am human, not because I am tired.
86. I give myself the grace I once withheld.
87. I honor my progress, not just my productivity.
88. I am a magnet for calm, grounded prosperity.
89. I can be loved in stillness as much as in action.
90. I receive joyfully and release freely.
91. I am worthy of support, seen and unseen.
92. My heart is expanding to hold abundance.
93. I am learning that peace is profitable.
94. I release the armor that blocks my blessings.
95. I am enough — now, always, again.
96. I let go of the urge to justify my rest.
97. I am reclaiming my right to softness.
98. It is safe to thrive beyond survival.
99. I was never undeserving; I was only afraid.
100. I receive life fully — and it receives me back.

Closing Note: Using the Deck for Deep Reconditioning

These mantras are not affirmations in the shallow sense — they are neural retraining tools. Each time you say one, you're telling your nervous system: *"This is the new normal."*

To deepen the practice:

- Write one mantra daily in your journal, adding a sentence about what it means for your current life.
- Speak one aloud in front of a mirror when you notice guilt or anxiety about receiving.
- Create physical "cards" — paper slips or a digital note deck — and shuffle them weekly.

Over time, you'll find that these words stop sounding like hope and start feeling like truth. That's when your worthiness core is no longer something you build — it's something you *live.*

Appendix B: The Self-Worth Ritual

Purpose of the Ritual

The *Self-Worth Ritual* is a structured yet flexible practice designed to retrain your nervous system to experience **deservingness as a state of safety, not performance**. Each element engages a different dimension of healing—physical grounding, emotional release, cognitive reframing, and spiritual remembrance—so that worthiness becomes embodied, not merely affirmed.

You can perform the full version weekly, or a condensed version daily in 10–15 minutes. Treat this not as another task, but as sacred maintenance—an energetic hygiene routine that restores the truth: *you are inherently enough.*

Preparation: Creating the Worth Space

Before beginning, clear a small area and gather symbolic tools that remind you of peace and prosperity. Suggestions:

- **Candle or soft light:** represents the flame of self-regard.
- **Bowl of water:** mirrors emotional depth and reflection.
- **Smooth stone or piece of earth:** anchors your body to stability.
- **Notebook or journal:** to record insights and sensations.
- **Optional scent or sound:** lavender oil, soft instrumental music, or silence.

Set the intention aloud:

"This space is safe. In this space, I do not have to earn my place. I am here to remember my worth."

The Four Pillars of the Self-Worth Ritual

Pillar 1 – Grounding the Body (Physical Safety)

Purpose: To calm the survival system that links stillness or abundance with danger.

Steps:

1. Stand or sit with both feet on the ground.
2. Inhale through your nose for a count of 4, exhale through your mouth for 6.
3. With each exhale, silently say, *"I am safe."*
4. Lightly press your palms against your thighs, feeling your solidity.
5. Visualize roots descending from your feet into the earth, carrying away shame, tension, and self-doubt.

Stay here for at least two minutes, letting the breath slow naturally. The goal is to anchor presence before moving inward.

Pillar 2 – Releasing the Old Contract (Emotional Cleansing)

Purpose: To dissolve subconscious vows such as "I must suffer to be loved" or "I have to give more than I receive."

Steps:

1. Place your hand over your heart and ask:
   "What false promise keeps me from feeling worthy today?"
2. Let an image, phrase, or sensation arise without forcing it.
3. Speak it aloud: *"I release the belief that ..."* (fill in the blank).
4. Exhale audibly, imagining the belief leaving your body.
5. Optional: Write the statement on paper and safely burn or tear it, saying,
   "This lesson is complete; I choose peace instead of proof."

Repeat this section whenever guilt or self-criticism resurfaces.

Pillar 3 – Receiving Activation (Cognitive & Energetic Re-patterning)

Purpose: To reprogram the brain's response from "alert" to "allow."

Steps:

1. Place both hands open on your lap, palms up.
2. Whisper: *"It is safe for me to receive."*
3. Visualize golden light pouring gently into your palms and traveling through your chest.
4. As you breathe, imagine this light expanding to fill your body.
5. Speak one mantra from Appendix A that feels resonant—example:
   "I can hold abundance without guilt."
6. Allow any warmth, tingling, or emotion to arise. These are signs that your body is practicing a new emotional posture: openness.

If tears or discomfort appear, stay kind. Your system is unlearning fear.

Pillar 4 – The Worth Declaration (Cognitive Integration)

Purpose: To solidify the new self-concept through language and ritual repetition.

Steps:

1. Look into a mirror or close your eyes and speak slowly:

"I am no longer earning my worth; I am living it."

2.Continue with three personal declarations beginning with *I am worthy of...*
Example: *I am worthy of calm mornings, consistent income, and loving boundaries.*

3.After each statement, breathe deeply and feel the truth land in your body.

4.Seal this section by saying,

"So it is. My worth is my foundation, not my reward."

3. Completion: The Rest Integration

After the four pillars, transition into stillness for 3–5 minutes. Lie down if possible. The goal is to let the nervous system experience safety *after* worthiness affirmation—a powerful rewiring step.

While resting, repeat silently:

"Doing nothing is holy. Receiving rest is receiving life."

Let the body memorize this calm. The ritual ends when you feel settled, not when a timer rings.

4. Optional Add-Ons by Season
To keep the practice alive throughout the year:

- **Winter:** Add warm tea or a blanket; focus on *rest and restoration.*
- **Spring:** Include flowers or greenery; emphasize *renewal and new opportunities.*
- **Summer:** Incorporate sunlight or outdoor air; focus on *visibility and joy.*
- **Autumn:** Use cinnamon, amber, or earthy tones; emphasize *harvest and gratitude.*

Each season reminds you that worthiness, like nature, has cycles—it expands, rests, regenerates.

5. Integrating the Ritual into Daily Life

1. **Micro-Moments:** Before meals or work, take one deep breath and think, *"I deserve nourishment."*
2. **Money Encounters:** Each time you receive payment, whisper, *"This is safety, not shame."*
3. **Before Sleep:** Place a hand on your heart and say, *"I am safe to rest."*
4. **When Triggered:** Ground, breathe, and silently repeat, *"Old fear, I recognize you. New safety, I choose you."*

Consistency creates neural familiarity; the more often you repeat these cues, the faster your worthiness becomes instinctive.

6. Journal Integration After the Ritual

Use your notebook to answer these reflection prompts:

- What sensations arose in my body during today's ritual?
- Did I resist any part of receiving? Why?
- What felt new, easier, or softer?
- Which mantra echoed loudest?
- One small way I can act from worthiness today is ...

Writing anchors emotion into cognition, bridging the spiritual with the practical.

7. Closing Benediction

At the end of each session, extinguish the candle or close the ritual space with gratitude. Say aloud:

"I honor the self who once believed she had to earn everything.
I honor the self who now knows she deserves rest, wealth, and love.
May this worth remain steady through all my seasons."

Sit for one last breath, acknowledging that the ritual itself is proof of transformation: you are tending to yourself as something valuable, not fixing something broken.

Final Note

Repetition is the architecture of belief. The more often you perform the *Self-Worth Ritual*, the less it will feel like an exercise and the more it will feel like truth.

Over time, you'll notice subtle shifts: decisions made with confidence, boundaries that hold, and opportunities that appear where scarcity once lived.

This ritual is your daily reminder that **you are not working toward worthiness—you are living from it.**

Message from the Author:

I hope you enjoyed this book, I love astrology and knew there was not a book such as this out on the shelf. I love metaphysical items as well. Please check out my other books:

-Life of Government Benefits

-My life of Hell

-My life with Hydrocephalus

-Red Sky

-World Domination:Woman's rule

-World Domination:Woman's Rule 2: The War

-Life and Banishment of Apophis: book 1

-The Kidney Friendly Diet

-The Ultimate Hemp Cookbook

-Creating a Dispensary(legally)

-Cleanliness throughout life: the importance of showering from childhood to adulthood.

-Strong Roots: The Risks of Overcoddling children

-Hemp Horoscopes: Cosmic Insights and Earthly Healing

- Celestial Hemp Navigating the Zodiac: Through the Green Cosmos

-Astrological Hemp: Aligning The Stars with Earth's Ancient Herb

-The Astrological Guide to Hemp: Stars, Signs, and Sacred Leaves

-Green Growth: Innovative Marketing Strategies for your Hemp Products and Dispensary

-Cosmic Cannabis

-Astrological Munchies

-Henry The Hemp

-Zodiacal Roots: The Astrological Soul Of Hemp

- **Green Constellations: Intersection of Hemp and Zodiac**

-Hemp in The Houses: An astrological Adventure Through The Cannabis Galaxy

-Galactic Ganja Guide

Heavenly Hemp
Zodiac Leaves
Doctor Who Astrology
Cannastrology
Stellar Satvias and Cosmic Indicas
Celestial Cannabis: A Zodiac Journey
AstroHerbology: The Sky and The Soil: Volume 1
AstroHerbology:Celestial Cannabis:Volume 2
Cosmic Cannabis Cultivation
The Starry Guide to Herbal Harmony: Volume 1
The Starry Guide to Herbal Harmony: Cannabis Universe: Volume 2
Yugioh Astrology: Astrological Guide to Deck, Duels and more
Nightmare Mansion: Echoes of The Abyss
Nightmare Mansion 2: Legacy of Shadows
Nightmare Mansion 3: Shadows of the Forgotten
Nightmare Mansion 4: Echoes of the Damned
The Life and Banishment of Apophis: Book 2
Nightmare Mansion: Halls of Despair
Healing with Herb: Cannabis and Hydrocephalus
Planetary Pot: Aligning with Astrological Herbs: Volume 1
Fast Track to Freedom: 30 Days to Financial Independence Using AI, Assets, and Agile Hustles
Cosmic Hemp Pathways
How to Become Financially Free in 30 Days: 10,000 Paths to Prosperity
Zodiacal Herbage: Astrological Insights: Volume 1
Nightmare Mansion: Whispers in the Walls
The Daleks Invade Atlantis
Henry the hemp and Hydrocephalus

10X The Kidney Friendly Diet
Cannabis Universe: Adult coloring book

Hemp Astrology: The Healing Power of the Stars

Zodiacal Herbage: Astrological Insights: Cannabis Universe: Volume 2

Planetary Pot: Aligning with Astrological Herbs: Cannabis Universes: Volume 2

Doctor Who: Convergence Protocol – The Replicator War

Nightmare Mansion: Curse of the Blood Moon

The Celestial Stoner: A Guide to the Zodiac

Cosmic Pleasures: Sex Toy Astrology for Every Sign

Hydrocephalus Astrology: Navigating the Stars and Healing Waters

Lapis and the Mischievous Chocolate Bar

Celestial Positions: Sexual Astrology for Every Sign

Apophis's Shadow Work Journal: **:** A Journey of Self-Discovery and Healing

Kinky Cosmos: Sexual Kink Astrology for Every Sign

Digital Cosmos: The Astrological Digimon Compendium

Stellar Seeds: The Cosmic Guide to Growing with Astrology

Apophis's Daily Gratitude Journal

Cat Astrology: Feline Mysteries of the Cosmos

The Cosmic Kama Sutra: An Astrological Guide to Sexual Positions

Unleash Your Potential: A Guided Journal Powered by AI Insights

Whispers of the Enchanted Grove

Cosmic Pleasures: An Astrological Guide to Sexual Kinks

369, 12 Manifestation Journal

Whisper of the nocturne journal(blank journal for writing or drawing)

The Boogey Book

Locked In Reflection: A Chastity Journey Through Locktober

Generating Wealth Quickly:How to Generate $100,000 in 24 Hours

Star Magic: Harness the Power of the Universe

The Flatulence Chronicles: A Fart Journal for Self-Discovery

The Doctor and The Death Moth

Seize the Day: A Personal Seizure Tracking Journal

The Ultimate Boogeyman Safari: A Journey into the Boogie World and Beyond

Whispers of Samhain: 1,000 Spells of Love, Luck, and Lunar Magic: Samhain Spell Book

Apophis's guides:Witch's Spellbook Crafting Guide for Halloween

Frost & Flame: The Enchanted Yule Grimoire of 1000 Winter Spells

The Ultimate Boogey Goo Guide & Spooky Activities for Halloween Fun

Harmony of the Scales: A Libra's Spellcraft for Balance and Beauty

The Enchanted Advent: 36 Days of Christmas Wonders

Nightmare Mansion: The Labyrinth of Screams

Harvest of Enchantment: 1,000 Spells of Gratitude, Love, and Fortune for Thanksgiving

The Boogey Chronicles: A Journal of Nightly Encounters and Shadowy Secrets

The 12 Days of Financial Freedom: A Step-by-Step Christmas Countdown to Transform Your Finances

Sigil of the Eternal Spiral Blank Journal

A Christmas Feast: Timeless Recipes for Every Meal

Holiday Stress-Free Solutions: A Survival Guide to Thriving During the Festive Season

Yu-Gi-Oh! Holiday Gifting Mastery: The Ultimate Guide for Fans and Newcomers Alike

Holiday Harmony: A Hydrocephalus Survival Guide for the Festive Season

Celestial Craft: The Witch's Almanac for 2025 – A Cosmic Guide to Manifestations, Moons, and Mystical Events

Doctor Who: The Toymaker's Winter Wonderland

Tulsa King Unveiled: A Thrilling Guide to Stallone's Mafia Masterpiece

Pendulum Craft: A Complete Guide to Crafting and Using Personalized Divination Tools

Nightmare Mansion: Santa's Eternal Eve

Starlight Noel: A Cosmic Journey through Christmas Mysteries

The Dark Architect: Unlocking the Blueprint of Existence

Surviving the Embrace: The Ultimate Guide to Encounters with The Hugging Molly

The Enchanted Codex: Secrets of the Craft for Witches, Wiccans, and Pagans

Harvest of Gratitude: A Complete Thanksgiving Guide

Yuletide Essentials: A Complete Guide to an Authentic and Magical Christmas

Celestial Smokes: A Cosmic Guide to Cigars and Astrology

Living in Balance: A Comprehensive Survival Guide to Thriving with Diabetes Insipidus

Cosmic Symbiosis: The Venom Zodiac Chronicles

The Cursed Paw of Ambition

Cosmic Symbiosis: The Astrological Venom Journal

Celestial Wonders Unfold: A Stargazer's Guide to the Cosmos (2024-2029)

The Ultimate Black Friday Prepper's Guide: Mastering Shopping Strategies and Savings

Cosmic Sales: The Astrological Guide to Black Friday Shopping

Legends of the Corn Mother and Other Harvest Myths

Whispers of the Harvest: The Corn Mother's Journal

The Evergreen Spellbook

The Doctor Meets the Boogeyman

The White Witch of Rose Hall's SpellBook

The Gingerbread Golem's Shadow: A Study in Sweet Darkness

The Gingerbread Golem Codex: An Academic Exploration of Sweet Myths

The Gingerbread Golem Grimoire: Sweet Magicks and Spells for the Festive Witch

The Curse of the Gingerbread Golem

10-minute Christmas Crafts for kids

Christmas Crisis Solutions: The Ultimate Last-Minute Survival Guide

Gingerbread Golem Recipes: Holiday Treats with a Magical Twist

The Infinite Key: Unlocking Mystical Secrets of the Ages

Enchanted Yule: A Wiccan and Pagan Guide to a Magical and Memorable Season

Dinosaurs of Power: Unlocking Ancient Magick

Astro-Dinos: The Cosmic Guide to Prehistoric Wisdom

Gallifrey's Yule Logs: A Festive Doctor Who Cookbook

The Dino Grimoire: Secrets of Prehistoric Magick

The Gift They Never Knew They Needed

The Gingerbread Golem's Culinary Alchemy: Enchanting Recipes for a Sweetly Dark Feast

A Time Lord Christmas: Holiday Adventures with the Doctor

Krampusproofing Your Home: Defensive Strategies for Yule

Silent Frights: A Collection of Christmas Creepypastas to Chill Your Bones

Santa Raptor's Jolly Carnage: A Dino-Claus Christmas Tale

Prehistoric Palettes: A Dino Wicca Coloring Journey

The Christmas Wishkeeper Chronicles

The Starlight Sleigh: A Holiday Journey

Elf Secrets: The True Magic of the North Pole

Candy Cane Conjurations

Cooking with Kids: Recipes Under 20 Minutes

Doctor Who: The TARDIS Confiscation

The Anxiety First Aid Kit: Quick Tools to Calm Your Mind

Frosty Whispers: A Winter's Tale

The Infinite Key: Unlocking the Secrets to Prosperity, Resilience, and Purpose

The Grasping Void: Why You'll Regret This Purchase

Astrology for Busy Bees: Star Signs Simplified

The Instant Focus Formula: Cut Through the Noise

The Secret Language of Colors: Unlocking the Emotional Codes

Sacred Fossil Chronicles: Blank Journal

The Christmas Cottage Miracle

Feeding Frenzy: Graboid-Inspired Recipes

Manifest in Minutes: The Quick Law of Attraction Guide

The Symbiote Chronicles: Doctor Who's Venomous Journey

Think Tiny, Grow Big: The Minimalist Mindset

The Energy Key: Unlocking Limitless Motivation

New Year, New Magic: Manifesting Your Best Year Yet

Unstoppable You: Mastering Confidence in Minutes

Infinite Energy: The Secret to Never Feeling Drained

Lightning Focus: Mastering the Art of Productivity in a Distracted World

Saturnalia Manifestation Magick: A Guide to Unlocking Abundance During the Solstice

Graboids and Garland: The Ultimate Tremors-Themed Christmas Guide

12 Nights of Holiday Magic

The Power of Pause: 60-Second Mindfulness Practices

The Quick Reset: How to Reclaim Your Life After Burnout

The Shadow Eater: A Tale of Despair and Survival

The Micro-Mastery Method: Transform Your Skills in Just Minutes a Day

Reclaiming Time: How to Live More by Doing Less

Chronovore: The Eternal Nexus

The Mind Reset: Unlocking Your Inner Peace in a Chaotic World
Confidence Code: Building Unshakable Self-Belief
Baby the Vampire Terrier
Baby the Vampire Terrier's Christmas Adventure
Celestial Streams: The Content Creator's Astrology Manual
The Wealth Whisperer: Unlocking Abundance with Everyday Actions
The Energy Equation: Maximize Your Output Without Burning Out
The Happiness Algorithm: Science-Backed Steps to Joyful Living
Stress-Free Success: Achieving Goals Without Anxiety
Mindful Wealth: The New Blueprint for Financial Freedom
The Festive Flavors of New Year: A Culinary Celebration
The Master's Gambit: Keys of Eternal Power
Shadowed Secrets: Groundhog Day Mysteries
Beneath the Burrow: Lessons from the Groundhog
Spring's Whispers: The Groundhog's Prediction
The Limitless Mindset: Unlock Your Untapped Potential
The Focus Funnel: How to Cut Through Chaos and Get Results
Bold Moves: Building Courage to Live on Your Terms
The Daily Shift: Simple Practices for Lasting Transformation
The Quarter-Life Reset: Thriving in Your 20s and 30s
The Art of Shadowplay: Building Your Own Personal Myth
The Eternal Loop: Finding Purpose in Repetition
Burrowing Wisdom: Life Lessons from the Groundhog
Shadow Work: A Groundhog Day Perspective
Love in Bloom: 5-Minute Romantic Gestures
The Shadowspell Codex: Secrets of Forbidden Magick
The Burnout Cure: Finding Balance in a Busy World
The Groundhog Prophecy: Unlocking Seasonal Secrets
Nog Tales: The Spirited History of Eggnog
Six More Weeks: Embracing Seasonal Transitions
The Lumivian Chronicles: Fragments of the Fifth Dimension

Money on Your Mind: A Beginner's Guide to Wealth
The Focus Fix: Breaking Through Distraction
January's Spirit Keepers: Mystical Protectors of the Cold
Creativity Unchained: Unlocking Your Wildest Ideas in 2025
Manifestation Mastery: 365 Days to Rewrite Your Reality
The Groundhog's Mirror: Reflecting on Change
The Weeping Angels' Christmas Curse
Burrowed in Time: A Groundhog Day Journey
Heartbeats: Poems to Share with Your Valentine
Dino Wicca: The Sacred Grimoire of Prehistoric Magick
Courage of the Pride: Finding Your Inner Roar
The Lion's Leap: Bold Moves for Big Results
Healthy Hustle: Achieving Without Overworking
Practical Manifesting: Turning Dreams into Reality in 2025
Jurassic Pharaohs: Unlocking the Magick of Ancient Egypt and Dino Wicca
The Happiness Equation: Small Changes for Big Joy
The Confidence Compass: Finding Your Inner Strength
Whispers in the Hollow: Tales of the Forgotten Beasts
Echoes from the Hollow: The Return of Forgotten Beasts
The Hollow Ascendant: The Rise of the Forgotten Beasts
The Relationship Reset: Building Better Connections
Mastering the Morning: How to Win the Day Before 8 AM
The Shadow's Dance: Groundhog Day Symbolism
Cupid's Kitchen: Quick Valentine's Day Recipes
Valentine's Day on a Budget: Love Without Breaking the Bank
Astrocraft: Aligning the Stars in the World of Minecraft
Forecasting Life: Groundhog Day Reflections

Bleeding Hearts: Twisted Tales of Valentine's Terror

Herbal Smoke Revolution: The Ultimate Guide to Nature's Cigarette Alternative

Winter's Wrath: The Complete Survival Blueprint for Extreme Freezes.

The Groundhog's Shadow: A Tale of Seasons
Burrowed Insights: Wisdom from the Groundhog
Sensual Strings: The Art of Erotic Bondage
Whispered Flames: Unlocking the Power of Fire Play
Forgotten Shadows: A Guide to Cryptids Lost to Time
Six Weeks of Secrets: Groundhog Day's Hidden Messages
Shadows and Cycles: Groundhog Day Reflections
The Art of Love Letters: Crafting the Perfect Message
Romantic Getaways at Home: Turning Your Space into Paradise
Purrfect Brews: A Cat Lover's Guide to Coffee and Companionship
The Groundhog's Wisdom: Timeless Lessons for Modern Life
The Shadow Oracle: Groundhog Day as a Predictor
Emerging from the Burrow: A Journey of Renewal
The Language of Love: Learning Your Partner's Love Style
Authorpreneur: The Ultimate Blueprint for Writing, Publishing, and Thriving as an Author
Weathering the Seasons: Groundhog Day Perspectives
Valentine's Day Magic: A Guide to Romantic Rituals
The Shadow Chronicles: Stories of Groundhog Day
Love and Laughter: Fun Games for Valentine's Day
AstroRealty: Unlocking the Stars for Property Success
The Groundhog's Path: A Guide to Seasonal Balance
Groundhog Day Diaries: Reflections in the Shadow
The Groundhog's Light: Illuminating the Path Ahead
Valentine's Traditions from Around the World
AI Wealth Revolution: Unlocking the Trillionaire Mindset
Love Rekindled: Reigniting Passion in Relationships
Single and Thriving: Self-Love on Valentine's Day
Emerald Legends: Mystical Tales of Ireland
Green Alchemy: Harnessing Nature's Magic
The Hearts of Horror: A Valentine's Day Nightmare

The Leprechaun's Guide to Wealth and Wisdom
Dancing with the Sidhe: Celebrating the Otherworld
Shamrocks and Shadows: Mysteries of the Green Isle
Emerald Energy: Harnessing Luck and Growth
The Gingerbread Golem's Valentine: A Sweetheart's Guide to Love and Enchantment
The Celtic Knot: Weaving Life and Destiny
Green Fire: Elemental Magic for St. Patrick's Day
Clover Chronicles: Finding Your Inner Luck
Ireland's Mystical Creatures: A Field Guide
Gingerbread Golem's Love Almanac
Prowl and Thrive: The Lion's Guide to Success
Love Alchemy: Transforming Your Life Through Heart Energy
WORLD DOMINATION: Woman's Rule 3:The New Life
The Midnight Rose: A Guide to Lunar Love Spells
The Forbidden Letters: Writing Your Own Love Prophecy
Luck and Lore: St. Patrick's Day for Modern Mystics
The Green Path: A Pagan Celebration of Renewal
The Dark Architect's Guide to Reprogramming Reality
Prankster's Paradise: A Guide to Harmless Hijinks
Manifest Your Reality: The Law of Attraction Simplified
The TARDIS Owner's Manual: Understanding the Doctor's Ship: *A complete guide to the TARDIS, its technology, secrets, and mysteries*
Starlit Romance: Astrology Secrets for Finding True Love
The Time Lord's Atlas: A Complete Guide to the Whoniverse: ***A breakdown of the locations, planets, and dimensions explored in Doctor Who***
Sweetheart Shadows: The Dark Side of Love and Attraction
February Fire: Reigniting Passion in Every Area of Life
The Self-Love Toolkit: 5 Ways to Embrace Who You Are
February Sparks: Ignite Your Dreams in 28 Days

March to Success: A 31-Day Action Blueprint
Ancient Paths: The 13 Sacred Principles of Dino Wicca
Echoes of Tomorrow: Navigating the AI Revolution
The Wellness Blueprint: Balancing Mind, Body, and Soul
Green Horizons: Sustainable Living for a Better Tomorrow
The AI Wealth Code: How to Make Millions with Automation
AI-Powered Creativity: Writing, Art, and Music for Profit
Extinction Rites: Rebirthing Your Soul Through Prehistoric Magick
Sacred Serpents tarot
Celestial Enchantment blank journal
Star Strains
Culinary Journeys: Exploring Global Flavors at Home
The Hollowvale Curse
The Hollowvale Harvest
The Egg of Transformation: Awakening Your Inner Power
Blooming Into Power: A Wiccan Guide to Spring Awakening
The Nightmare Nexus: The Third Doctor's Perilous Haunting
Digital Detox: Reclaiming Your Life in a Connected World
Ostara's Path: Walking the Spiral of Renewal
The Sacred Hare
Financial Freedom: Building Wealth in the Modern Age
Spring's Cauldron: Stirring the Waters of Change
The Hollowvale Pact
Quantum Consciousness: The Science of Reality Shifting
The Hollowvale Hunger
The Sacred Waters Within: A Witch's Guide to Hydrocephalus Magick
The Raven's Nest: Building a Life of Unshakable Stability
AI and the Human Mind: The Future of Intelligence
The Hollowvale Reckoning
Timeless Love: Building and Maintaining Lasting Relationships

The Raven's Roar: Unlocking Unstoppable Confidence
Raven Sight: Awakening Intuition and Inner Wisdom
The Butterfly Effect: Small Changes, Big Transformations
Taming the Boogeyman: How to Conquer Your Inner Fears
The Magick of Green: Awakening Earth's Energy in You
The Entrepreneurial Mindset: Secrets to Business Success
The Hollowvale End
The Shadow Luck Ritual: Reclaiming Power from Your Dark Side
Spring Magick for Beginners: A Simple Guide to Seasonal Energy Work
Doctor Who: The Hollowvale Conundrum
The March of Miracles: Unlocking Synchronicities in Spring
Unveiling the Cosmos: A Guide to Stargazing and Space Exploration
The Ultimate Guide to Surviving an Economic Collapse
The AI Gold Rush: How to Profit from the AI Revolution
Bastet's Shadow: The Hidden Power of Feline Magick
The Bastet Codex: Unlocking the Goddess's Magickal Secrets
Purring Spells: Harnessing Bastet's Healing Frequencies
Bastet's Nine Lives: Rebirth, Transformation, and Immortality Spells
Primal Currents: Hydrocephalus Magick in the Path of Dino Wicca
The Digital Gold Rush: Mastering E-Commerce and Online Sales
Future Shock: Adapting to the Next Decade of Change
The Quantum Mindset: Think Like a Billionaire
Sacred Motherhood: Awakening the Divine Feminine Within
The Mother's Spellbook: Enchantments for Love, Protection, and Prosperity
The Witch's Guide to Parenting: Raising Empowered and Intuitive Children

The Magick of Motherhood: Reclaiming Your Power Through Rituals
The Pagan Path to Self-Love: A Goddess's Guide to Worth and Confidence
Wild Woman Magick: Unleashing Your Primal Power
The Money Magnet Blueprint: Unlocking Unlimited Wealth
Biohacking 101: Unlock Your Body's Full Potential
The Wild Father: A Pagan Guide to Strength and Wisdom
The Sacred Masculine: Unlocking Your Inner Power
The Druid's Compass
The Warrior's Mindset
The Father's Fire
Odin's Path
Ancestral Bonds
The House That Whispers
The Magician's Code
The Wild Hunt
The Green Man's Path
The Altar of Success
The Shadow and the Sword
The High Priestess's Guide to Energy Healing
The Lunar Mother
The Sacred Self-Care Grimoire
The Womb Wisdom Codex
The Wheel of the Mother
The Witch's Guide to Manifestation
The Q2 Reset
The Ultimate Guide to AI-Powered Passive Income
Escape the 9-5
AI Feline Fortunes
The Tear-Stained Grimoire
Razorblade Runes
Cemetery Sirens

The Midnight Wristwatch
The Town That Forgets
AI Horror & Creepypasta
The Hollow Frequency
The Breach Echo
The Quiet Between Worlds
The Sigil of Tharan-Khul
Summon the Vault of Y'ha'ten
The Becoming Codex
The Profit of Az'ra-nar
The Drowned Logos
Echoes of the Eldritch Will
The Deep Ledger
Necronomicon of Networth
Covenant of the Wealthwyrm
The Whisperer's Manifesto
The Rites of Azh-K'luth
The Ark of the Crawling Coin
The Tithe of Shadows
Inkheart Abyss
The Timewinds of Y'ha-nthlei
The Spiral Labyrinth of Azag-Nirrh
The Gallifreyan Heresy of the Black Pharaoh
The Psalms of Nyog-Sotha
Black Rain Alchemy
The Infinite Maw
The Entropic Blueprint
The Oracle of Sh'guul
The Book of Breach
The Drowned Saint's Testament
Dreamcraft of the Sleeper God
The Silence Market
Cthonomics: The Dark Wealth Algorithm

Invocation of the Ten-Eyed King
Wealthbound to the Wyrm Below
Become the Unnameable
Codex of the Sovereign Flame
Rituals of Relentless Becoming
The Shadow Ascends
The Eyes Beneath You
The Will That Wakes Worlds
Silence Is a Weapon
The Mirror That Screams
The Whisper Between Moments
The Mind That Devours Fear
The Myth of the Finished Self
The Architect of Your Madness
The Voice You've Buried
The Discipline of Madness
Stormborn: Awakening Your Inner Tempest
The Mind That Ate Time
Unbind Your Becoming
The Pact You Owe Yourself
The Devourer's Diet
The Acid That Carves the Path
The Tower You Must Burn
The Breath Between Worlds
Speak Like the Deep
The Labyrinth Within
The Spine of the Sea God
Rejection Is a Portal
The Crown You Refused
The Scar Is the Spell
The Lightless Flame
The Habit of Becoming Horrific
ChickenJockey Chaos

The Gatekeeper Within
You Are Not Your Name
The Compass of the Mad
The Archive of Unsent Letters
What the Mirror Can't Show You
The Knife You Needed
Worship Nothing, Become Everything
The Other Voice
The Body the World Forgot
The Vein of the Void
The Black Bone Codex
The Puzzle of the Hidden Self (Millennium Puzzle)
The Eye That Sees the Lie *(Millennium Eye)*
The Ring of Return (Millennium Ring)
The Rod of Relentless Will ***(Millennium Rod)***
The Tally of the Soul (Millennium Tauk/Necklace)
The Key to the Locked Timeline (Millennium Key)
The Scale of Sacred Decisions (Millennium Scales)
Inferno Bites: The UnOfficial Minecraft Lava Cookbook
Rot in the Attic
Prana: The Hidden Force of Your Infinite Self
The Shadow Realm Within: Transforming Darkness Into Destiny
The Borderland Collapse
Claws of Protection: Bastet's Defensive Magick
Mr. Ring-a-Ding's Madness
Yugioh Astrology: Celestial Deckcraft and Duel Destiny (2026–2027 Edition)
The Seal You Signed: Unlocking the Power You Once Feared
The Puzzle of Infinite Minds: Unlocking the Mentalism Hidden Within
The Eye That Mirrors the All: Secrets of Inner Reflection
Doctor Who: The Toymaker's Broadcast

The Rod of Eternal Flow: Commanding the Currents of Vibration
Golden Eyes of Bastet: Enhancing Psychic Vision
The Key of Dual Forces: Balance Within the Polarity
The Scales of Living Rhythm: Timing the Dance of Life
The Necklace of Hidden Cause: Weaving the Webs of Fate
The Ring of Secret Masters: Rising Through the All Within All
Daggers of the Dying Deep
Bastet's Wealth and Fortune Magick: Prosperity Rituals of the Goddess
The Tide that Speaks
The Scrolls of Petosiris: 13 Rituals from the Feathered Eye
Petosiris and the Living Plague of Osirion
Feline Fire: Bastet's Passion and Love Magick
The Star Altar of Petosiris
Bastet's Whiskers: Supernatural Sensory Magick
The Bastet Grimoire
Feeding the Shadows
The Mouthless Prayer
The Spiral Wound
Becoming the Ibis: Lessons from Petosiris's Mind
The Crimson Coven: Cola Magick for Sweet Dominion
Sacred Cat's Paw
The Soda Zodiac: A Flavor for Every Sign
Covenant of the Crawling Flame
The Ink of Ish'Zur
Frothroot: The Thirst That Ate the World
The Golden Glyphs of Prosperity
The Etherbind Codex
Echoes of the Resistance: Reclaiming the You That Survived
Harnessed Minds: Breaking Free from Mental Control
The Eyes in the Smoke

Rootwake: The Carbon Covenant
Skitter Logic: Unlearning the Fear That Built You
Doctor Who: The World That Froths
Rootwake: The Fizz That Rewrites Flesh
Rootwake: Frothfather of the World
The Holly Pact: Blood Beneath the Mistletoe
The 2nd Mass Principle: Building Unbreakable Tribes
Web of Wits: A Survival Guide to Encounters with Anasi the Spider (Aunt Nancy)
The Hexbreaking Handbook: Effective Spells to Remove Curses
Pop Alchemy: Transform Your Life One Sip at a Time
The Mason Code: Leading in Unleadable Times
Petosiris and the Fifth Chamber of Thoth
The Ether Seed Within
The Parent of Tomorrow
Petosiris's Pyramid of Perpetual Wealth
Unlearn the World
Grimoire of the Hollow Tongue
Zodiac Weeds: Finding Your Strain Through the Stars
Aquarius Rises in the Bank
The Sugar God's Smile
The Skinclock Reversal: Biohacking the Face of Time
Debtburn: How to Obliterate What You Owe Forever
The Ice Cream Oracle: What Your Cone Says About Your Future
Silence Is Sovereignty: The Power of Being Unreadable
The Wind That Whispers Through Stone
Path of the Four Directions
Doctor Who: The Maestro's Symphony of Endings
Oxygen Grail: Breathing to Undo the Clock
Zodiacal Collapse: When Stars Devour Time
Teachings from the Red Sand Silence

Doctor Who: Omega – The Broken Equation

Memory Wipe Your Past: Start Over Like a MiB

Mitochondria Prime: Ignite the Core of Youth

A Nest of Roaches

Grub from the Galaxy: MiB Recipes You'll Never Forget

Whiskers of Power: Bastet's Guide to Inner Sovereignty

The Gift Must Cost Them: Negotiation Through Unequal Exchange

The Worm Guys' Wealth Code: Hustle Like an Alien

Bug Out: The Edgar Method for Ruthless Goal Setting

Weaving Life with Spiderwoman's Pattern

Doctor Who: The Rani's Renaissance

How to Get a Job (If You're a Puppygirl)

Speak Through Others: The Art of Proxy Power

T-Rex Your Trauma: Reclaim the Power of Your Primal Self

The Black Briefcase: How MiB Stay Wealthy in Silence

The Thirst Beyond Reason: Understanding Diabetes Insipidus From the Inside Out

Backwoods Witchcraft for Billionaires: The Pagan Path from Dirt Roads to Gold Roads

The Moonshine Grimoire: Fermented Spells for Abundance

The Nameless Geometry

The Wraith's Mixtape: Spellcasting with Songs of Sorrow

The Gallifreyan Gentleman: Silent Wealth, Sonic Confidence, and the Doctor's Code of Living

Sugar Water Confidence

Dino Totems: Spirit Guides from Earth's First Gods

Pumpkin Sigils & Ritual Smoke

The Hózhó Compass

The Distortus Discipline – Order from Inner Mutation

Witchcraft for the Cold-Blooded Soul

Moonlight Over the Blessingway

Water, Interrupted: When the Body Forgets How to Hold On

Deformed but Divine: Embracing Your Asymmetry
Hexes in the Henhouse: The Farm Witch's Guide to Power
The Reversed Flame: A Grimoire of Inverted Power
Salt, Cells, and Sanity: Reclaiming Balance with Diabetes Insipidus
King of the Broken: Crowning the Flawed Self
Moonlight Scars: Emo Moon Magick and the Art of Lunar Sorrow
Noose Spells: Magick of the Hanging Rope
The Goth Cathedral: Rituals of the Broken and Beautiful
The Cretaceous Codex: Dino Spirits and Fossil Magick
The Turkey Bones Ritual
Nine Lives of Manifestation: Unlocking Bastet's Reality Codes
Chaos Muscles: Building Strength from Twisted Pain
Emo Blood Magick: The Veins of Power
The 3AM Flood: Nighttime Urination, Sleep Loss, and the DI Spiral
The Silence Between the Stars
The Lemon Method: Sour Your Way to Success
Starlit Sovereign
The Rite of Twelve Gates: Walking the Gates of the Duat.
Cornbread and Conjure: Recipes for Riches and Rootwork
The Black Rose Rituals: Emo Love Spells and Obsession Magick
The Eternal Goodbye: Death Magick and Rebirth Rituals
Sinkrot: The Drain That Remembers
The Hybrid Mindset: Thinking Beyond Evolution
Bone Dry: Navigating Dehydration Before It Breaks You
Wreathcraft: Winter Sigils and Yuletide Spells
The Rite of Twelve Mouths
S'mores of the Damned: Haunted Recipes for Halloween Night

Rethink the Drink: A Beverage Survival Guide for DI Warriors

The Shadow Chord: Guitar Magick and Sonic

Malformed Yet Majestic: Leading When You Feel Wrong Inside

The Cursed Diary: Ink-Stained Spells of the Emo Soul

Anxiety Off Switch: Emergency Reset for a Fried Nervous System

The Energy Heist: How to Take Back Your Life from Drainers

Beyond the Bathroom: Rebuilding Your Social Life With DI

Coyote's Gift for Decision Makers

Ghoul-Goo: Spooky S'mores You'll Die For

Echoes in the Mirror: Scrying and Self-Destruction Magick

Thread and Thorn: Stitching Spells from Rural Cloth

The Mogwai Mind: Building Untouchable Wealth from Small Ideas

Be Your Own Guide: Trust Your Inner Compass

Hormones in Chaos: The Endocrine Puzzle of Diabetes Insipidus

ChronoCleanse: Detox Your Biological Timeline

The Limb You Hide Is the One That Saves You

Leaves, Bones, and Whisper Spells

The Dinosaur Mindset: Prehistoric Tactics for Modern Wealth

Clawing Back Control: A Bastet Method for Boundaries and Empowerment

Samhain Codes of the Forgotten

Orange Alchemy: The Autumnal Spellbook

Monster Within, Master Without

The Sigil That Sleeps

Hearthcraft: Yule Hearth Sigils and Winter Warmth Spells

Temple of the Purring Moon: Rituals from Bastet's Lineage

When the Earth Remembers Your Footsteps

Food for Mood: Eat to Heal Depression, Not Just Survive It
Witch of the Kudzu Vine: Southern Pagan Wealth Secrets
The Invisible Diagnosis: Advocating for Yourself With DI
The Coffin's Lullaby: Sleep Magick and Nightmares as Portals
Ashes of the Will: Rituals for Erasing the Self
The Fracture Rite: Shattering the Magickal Core
Funeral Candles: The Art of Emo Flame Magick
The Black Grimoire: A Blank Ritual for Writing in Absence
Phantom Thirst: A Halloween Survival Guide for Diabetes Insipidus
The Hollow Crown: Emo Royalty and Magick of the Outcast King
Sandpainting for the Soul
Falling Into Balance: Using the Extra Hour to Recalibrate Life
100 Southern Superstitions That Still Work
The DI Child: A Parent's Guide to Raising Hydrated, Happy Kids
The Jungle of Shame: Escaping the Hidden Lab of Doubt
The Witch's Toast: S'mores Spells and Creepy Confections
The Hoodoo Pantry: Spells from the Mason Jar
The Immortal Fortune: Secret Wealth Lessons from Captain Jack Harkness
The Specter's Embrace: Magick for Channeling Ghostly Lovers
Grateful Waters: A Thanksgiving Survival Guide for Diabetes Insipidus
The Seizure Gospel
Harvestbind: Autumn Sigils and Samhain Spells
Doctor Who: The Algorithmic Awakening
Silent Nights, Steady Waters: A Christmas Survival Guide for Diabetes Insipidus
The Extra Hour Effect: How One Hour Can Transform Everything

Blade Between the Breaths

Running with the Mountain Shadows

Echoes of the Failed Experiment – Becoming a Living Legacy

Swamp Witches & River Ghosts: Real Southern Hauntings

Cornbread Prophecies: Magical Recipes from a Southern Table

Doctor Who: The Signal in the Star

Bloomcraft: Spring Sigils and Equinox Enchantments

Vanisher: How to Disappear from the Internet Without Losing Your Life

The Ultimate Christmas Cookie Cookbook

The Unbreakable Parent: How to Mentally Survive Raising Kids in a Broken World

Time Debt: How to Reclaim the Hours You Didn't Know You Lost

One Month, One Million: Unconventional Cash Creation Tactics

Doctor Who: The Cyber Conversion Protocol

Black Friday Frenzy: The Art of Finding Hidden Online Deals

The Grimoire Buried Under the Apple Tree

Digital Couponing Masterclass: Your Step-by-Step Guide to Black Friday Savings

The Fire Inside the Flint

Shadows on the Ceiling: The Emo Guide to Astral Magick

The Bone-Eaters Beneath Us

Black Friday Bundle Blueprint: Creating Irresistible Product Packages for Maximum Sales

Thirteen Nights of Unbinding

Doctor Who: Engines of Influence

Pumpkin Spice Alchemy: Recipes of Fire and Frost

When Raptor Met Rexy: Prehistoric Lessons in Wild Romance

Oblivion's Candle: Burn the Path Behind You

Campfire Curses and Chocolate: A Halloween S'mores Grimoire
The Wallet That Wasn't Mine: Breaking Free from Inherited Scarcity
The Cola Zodiac: What Your Fizz Says About Your Fate
Frostfire Fortune: Unlocking Winter's Hidden Prosperity
Signal Jamming: Detox Your Brain from Info Overload
The Dust of the Forgotten Rite
The Golden Cat Sigils: Drawing Power in Bastet's Name
Mud Magick: The Prosperity of Getting Dirty
Savory Spicefall: Beyond the Pumpkin Pie
Pumpkin Spice Apothecary Kitchen
The Pumpkin Spice Economy: Turning Trends into Billions
The Ember Veil: 13 Nights of Fire Magick
Financial Freeze: When Earning Triggers Panic
The Gingerbread Alchemist: Sweet Recipes with a Twist
Biosynth Power: Programming Yourself from Scratch
Echoes from the Talking Circle
Truffle Alchemy: Fungus of Fortune
Spores of Power: The Truffle Witch's Handbook
Doctor Who: The Tower That Speaks
The Mycelium Veil: Truffle Magick Unbound
Broke But Ashamed: Healing the Shame Wound of Debt
The Evergreen Mind: Growth Through Winter Stillness
The Black Veil Truffle Rite
The Voice Beneath Symbols
Witchlight on the Bayou: Swamp Spells for Sovereignty
I Grew Up Poor and Now I Sabotage My Success
The Lantern of Hollow Souls
Shutdown Survival: A Citizen's Guide to Thriving When Government Stops
When Abundance Feels Like a Threat: Healing the Hidden Fears of Enough

The Scarecrow Grimoire
Owls of the October Veil
Candlewax and Curses: A Halloween Spellbook
Excavating the Inner Fossil – Transforming Fossilized Thoughtforms into Tools of Power
The Yule Witch's Spellbook: Magick for the Holiday Season
Haunted Christmas: Ghost Stories for Winter Nights
The Christmas Survival Guide: Thriving Through the Chaos
The Bone Orchard Rites
Haunted Commerce: The Ghost in the Marketplace
When Money Triggers the Inner Child
Silent Night with the Silence: A Christmas Thriller
The Lightning Crown: Living and Leading Through Seizures
TARDIS Tidings: Festive Stories from the Whoniverse
Autumn Reset: Slowing Down Without Falling Behind
The Trillion Dollar Soul: Rewriting the Currency of Reality
Truffle Eclipse Magick
Micro-Manifestations: Quick Magick That Works
5-Minute Rituals for Busy Witches
The Marshmallow Massacre: Halloween Treats with a Sinister Twist
Blood and Blackberry Thorns
Magickal Mornings: Rituals for a Blessed Christmas Day
Embers of the All-Hallows Fire
The Pumpkin Market Collapse
The Hour You Gained: Transforming Time Into Power
The Chamber Must Be Sealed: Mastering the Power of Controlled Access
The Cursed Manuscript of Petosiris
The Festive Hearth: Creating Holiday Traditions
Darkness Rising: Thriving as Nights Grow Longer
Harvesting Time: Turning the Year's End Into Your New Beginning

Petosiris and the 13th Zodiac Key
Wagewound: When Paychecks Become Identity Prisons
Walls That Watch
The Silent Feast: Rituals of Power in the Longest Night
The Distortus Legacy : Becoming a Deformed King in a Perfect World
The Hollow Masks
The Gratitude Furnace: Forging Gold from Thanks
Feast of Inner Gold: Eating for Energy and Enlightenment
Haunted Commerce: The Season of Spending Spirits
Fear Bonds: How Panic Creates Profit
Black Friday E-Commerce Playbook: Sales Tactics to Skyrocket Your Holiday Revenue
Budgeting for Black Friday: A Holiday Savings Planner
Haunting the Harvest Moon
The Warrior's Water: Emergency Preparedness for People With DI
The First Sip of the Year: A New Year's Survival Guide for Diabetes Insipidus
Doctor Who: The Thirteenth Node
The Unseen Struggle: Mental Health, Anxiety, and Chronic Thirst
The Hearth's Hidden Ledger: Counting Energies as Currency
The Gift Alchemist: Turning Any Offering Into Gold
The Papyrus of the Bound Spirit
The Magick of Leftovers: Transmutation in the Fridge
Frost and Fortune: Christmas Wealthcraft for the Modern Magus
Last-Minute Gifts: Creative Ideas on a Budget
10 Secrets to Surviving Holiday Crowds
The Witch's Dow Jones
The Witches' Graveyard Shift
Pumpkin Sigils: Carving Rites for Midnight Power

The Secret Shopper's Black Friday Guide: How to Get Early Access and VIP Deals

Fever in the Foundation

The Neuralyzer Reset: Reprogram Your Morning Routine

Lightning Lessons of the White Painted Woman

The Enchanted Snowflake

The Magic Sip: Surviving Disney Parks with Diabetes Insipidus

The One Who Draws Through You

Santa's Secrets: A Magical Holiday Planner

Silent Bells, Loud Miracles: Self-Help for the Season of Stillness

The Sugar Spell Codex: Confectionary Magick of Christmas

Autumn Hexcraft: Fallen Leaves, Fallen Barriers

Sleep Like a Fortress: Build a Life Where Insomnia Can't Survive

Nowhere Was Ever Home

Christmas Under the Stars: A Celestial Holiday Guide

Rentproof: How to Never Be Evicted Again

Workless: Escape the 9-5 Without Being Broke

The Gilded Gift: A Wealth Altar for Christmas Morning

The Black Friday Grimoire

The Hollowing: Ceremonies of Spiritual Collapse

Doctor Who: The Nameless Signal

Where the Eagle Hides His Courage

The Dwarf Tyrant's Ascent: Claiming Power in a World of Giants

The Currency of the Dead: Trading with Spectral Bankers

The Icebound Witch: Survival and Magick in the Cold

The Emergency Money Mind: Constant Crisis, Zero Calm

Thirst & Roses: A Valentine's Survival Guide for Diabetes Insipidus

Springing Into Clarity: Mastering the Energy Shift of Daylight Saving

Speed of the Nanotyrant: Agile Strategies for Life's Hunt

The 90-Day Reset: A Science-Backed Guide to Reinvent Yourself Before the New Year

The Coil of Thorns

Timegates Unleashed

Dopamine Fasting 2.0: Rewiring Your Brain in a World of Overstimulation

The Nanotyrannus Mutation: Embracing Your Differentiated Form

Unwritten January: How to Use the Blank Page of the Year to Re-Author Your Life

Feast of the Forgotten Spirits: Ancestor Magick for the Holidays

The Burnout Codex: A System for Thriving Beyond Stress

Get Some Tarot cards: https://www.makeplayingcards.com/sell/apophis-occult-shop

Get some shirts: https://www.bonfire.com/store/apophis-shirt-emporium/

Instagrams:
@apophis_enterprises,
@apophisbookemporium,
@apophisscardshop
Twitter: @apophisenterpr1
Tiktok:@apophisenterprise
Youtube: @sg1fan23477
Hive: @sg1fan23477
CheeLee: @SG1fan23477

Podcast: Apophis Chat Zone: https://open.spotify.com/show/5zXbrCLEV2xzCp8ybrfHsk?si=fb4d4fdbdce44dec

Newsletter: https://apophiss-newsletter-27c897.beehiiv.com/

If you want to support me or see posts of other projects that I have come over to: **buymeacoffee.com/mpetchinskg**

I post there daily several times a day

Get your Dinowicca or Christmas themed digital products, especially Santa Raptor songs and other musics. Here: **https://sg1fan23477.gumroad.com**

Apophis Yuletide Digital has not only digital Christmas items, but it will have all things with Dinowicca as well as other Digital products.

www.ingramcontent.com/pod-product-compliance
Lightning Source LLC
LaVergne TN
LVHW022006200926
848481LV00007B/2267